Derivative

Patrick Johnson

BookLeaf Publishing

India | USA | UK

Presentation by *BookLeaf Publishing*

Web: www.bookleafpub.com

E-mail: info@bookleafpub.com

ISBN: 978-93-5744-931-1

First edition 2022

DEDICATION

For my mum and dad. Thank you for making me both question this strange world and treat it with compassion.

Cicadas

Loss is that firm lot of humanity.
Unaware of Pluto's dark enterprise,
Lover's folly, divine finality.
Unsuspecting mayflies self-aggrandised.
Youth is nothing but Persephone's fruit,
Swaying leaves amid the looming autumn.

Forlorn bells of a clock tower toll and
With each passing tick devours light, legion
And bliss. Wisdom of insidious sand
Flowing in the hourglass. Orphean dread,
Sight denied. Foolish as Tithon's first dawn,
Meek and mild as a lamb, cashmere forgone.

Solitary sails voyage to eyrie
Byzantium. A dissenting sunset,
Searching in vain among funerary
Sheets for a long omitted silhouette.
Why couldn't we be like the cicadas,
Pardoned from eulogised ephemera?

Imago

The black dog insidiously looms like an
oncoming tempest, lightning flashes for
Eyes and gnashing bleak clouds for jowls. Each
drip of rain a drop of poison.
All flavour of life turns to ash in the mouth of
the leper.
Belphegor's saccharine succour a tempting
Nourishment amid the drab but offers no true
pause.
The patient cries out for a cure, fixed to the mast
as the sailors row plaintiff. He
Screams Restitution to ears willingly clogged
with meek lamb's wool and
Hands cleansed of calluses like Pilate's.

A butterfly dreams of caterpillars as stain
Glass wings flutter amid the opaque
Metamorphosis. A sapling reminisces of the
dead
Elm. One dying soul gives birth to a second, but
even then that black
Dog Cerberus chases heedlessly its promised
headless
Convict, howling sweet sorrows like a siren in
the night. The

Runaway is Theseus' ship. How much change
until he is no longer himself?
Grieve the death, the broken glass cannot
reverse its shattering.

Now- follow that steadfast dove as it carves a
Path through the cavernous chrysalis to the
Imago, just as Beatrice led Dante through limbo.
Dissonance resolved, rise a phoenix from
Charon's denial. Sit dry in the hurricane's eye
and remember
That foul black dog guides only to stains on
ruined rocks, and threatens
Coalescence with their wet headstone blemishes
And tongues of obol.

Blue Pill

Daybreak cracks like chipped stone. "It's hotter
than it used to be" say the suit and tie prophets.
Two pill bottles wave from behind the mirror.
One pill will make you grow, the other wrinkles
the
Head. But the red pill tastes like radio static, and
the blue matches my boots. Swallow the dun
Dysthymia. Everything will be okay.

Supplicant beggars, tramps and mendicants all
clutch to winged crucifixes. Clad in faux brown
robes,
Deny the outstretched stigmata. "That is not a
widow's mite but a bag of snakes at your feet"
the
Black doves grin, and exchange their change for
a double shot of caffeine. An advertisement for
Superannuation plays on the billboard.
Everything will be okay.

Scroll through the pornographic media as Rome
melts like Dali clocks and praise those heroes
Fighting the flames. The new charity of a
thumbs up a poor substitute for helping hands.
Turn the

Blind eye to parliament petitions. "Why do they
have to be so preachy?" Lock the vanity of
new-age
Idols and replace the blaze with family photos.
Everything will be okay.

The brave lamb bleats "how dare you?" to the
blind, deaf and muted. She plucked a raven's eye
like
A vinegar onion for verisimilitude, but they
blinded their eyes with Founding Fathers and the
heads
Of queens. "It's not that simple" margins reply
from behind red-taped mouths, and the lamb's
wool
Drowns in cigarette tar. Everything will be okay.

Legacies

How can sons bear their father's legacy?
Only sons uphold the king's divine rite.
Only men can preserve posterity.

A mother's love near saved Persephone,
But Heracles should sustain Goya's bite.
How can sons bear their father's legacy?

Pendulum cuckoos of lost revelry,
Yet Thomas urged to fight the dying light.
Only men can preserve posterity.

Cain claimed by patriarch's rivalry,
Hamlet poisoned by ouroboros spite.
How can sons bear their father's legacy?

Christ stigmatised by a thorned prophecy,
Adam's curse haemorrhaged in angel flight.
Only men can preserve posterity.

Oaks- great to sapling- felled eternity
Thrones buried by poppy gardens bleached
white.
How can sons bear their father's legacy?
Only men can preserve posterity.

Day Break

Morning's rhapsody streams through the blinds
like a river through a grate.
Outside, sparrows cuddle on white blossom
branch tops. Fuck the lark!
Tease me with all the nothings I rambled in
dream. Savour the knotted tresses.
Toes escape the polar bear duvet and are mauled
by the dawn frost. She hauls her feet to rest on
my thigh- they burn like little icicles, freezing
their lover's brand into the flesh.

Red Tape

Quick! Silence the wails with red tape. Blind the
needle with thread and sew shut the lips like
breaching dolphins.
Oh, we're sorry, haven't you heard? Paperwork
is progress.

Daughter

She's blind, clearly, to the pride in your eye, to
the yellow of her words. Every
syllable of her day you dulcify and trace along,
sounding out the sounds
like you had never heard the words before. Only
when the fall rises and clouds clear
does she visit, sprouting from the earth like a
sunflower singing rhapsodies of a maiden's
veneer.

Maybe it's because your memory is faint. Those
same seasons left. Greyscale, faded Polaroids.
Maybe it's because you're a saint. It was Mary
who plucked the dogwood splinters.
Keep the understanding on the highest shelf. It
will remain a sweater that she'll grow
into when she's old enough for the loom.
Subjugate the knowledge, pin it with thread.
One visit she says that there's not much to tell,
but you insist. A boy? You snicker together, then
she crawls into her den in search of private
spaces that burn like a kiln. The clay aspect is
Botoxed.

The boy was no boy at all but an oval-cut cuff.
You said you could never be happier for her-
liar.
She laughs at your tears- thought they were
happy- but the streams were a watercolour
portrait.
No more spring. The bees have wintered. The
beau talks more- the only way you can hear
about her day. She used to share it with you. The
phone calls stink of despair, so you stop. It hurts
to let the bird fly the nest. She only returns on
holidays, when she's not with his parent's. At
least she calls on your birthday? When she
remembers that is. She's so busy these days.
Every day's the same. Choose your outfit, pick
at the food, the occasional fuck, sleep. You drink
a little more than you used. Just enough so that it
isn't a problem. Just enough to sleep.
And in your dreams you smile like you used to-
the toothless grin opens and dances like a
ballerina.
Stars of light break through the stone lids- a
cinema of the spring she used to bring.

Dear Dead Elm

Dear dead elm,
I weep that I never knew you. My life sprang
from yours as
the acorn from the oak. But when
you fell I was only a boy and couldn't grasp
your sovereignty.

Children often frolic
among your carcass in the Park, but even
cemeteries are
adorned in denial blooms.
Did you know that birds still flock to your
wrinkly wooden limbs?

That they delight
on their hopeful feather? The sparrows dance
and preen in ignorance
like raucous schoolboys copying
one another's work. At dawn they gather on the
beaches of

Gallipoli to honour
you. They know not of how you held up worlds,
Yggdrasil- that in the end

You asked what lips
you kissed and where and why as if your roots
bathed in the river Lethe.

If you could
see this legacy would you be content? Would
those limbs that ached and
leaves that left one
autumn like petulant hairs never to return now
be soothed in the scion's inheritance?

Battler

Look at the senator sipping a pint in his fluro vest.
So unlike a snake to be so visible.

Transplant

The tethers to the trees have slackened,
the connection to the forests weakened.
So many families torn down for progress;
sham screensavers as the roots evanesce.
Flee the false obelisks of brick like birds
migrating home. Escape the glum landlords,
reject the idolatry of plastic
apples, clowns, and guns as a monastic
culls the material. Rediscover
apostolic woods like a lost lover.
Transplant the potted toes into the soil.
Prune the three piece and let the limbs unfurl.

Old Friends

That's where we used to play and laugh and
scream.
Two swings swam through the air; scoop the
legs up to get higher.
You jumped the furthest, but I was quicker on
the monkey bars.
Our mothers laughed with pearl grins, then
called us over for hot chips
and we flocked like seagulls.

Now the only sway of the swings is from the
winter wind.
The slide is pale. It used to be yellow like yolk. I
tried to call the other day
but you were busy. That's how we both are now.
That's how everyone is now.
Maybe one day soon we can go back- I'll bring
the chips if you take the time.
Maybe one day we could be like we used to.
Maybe.

Teacher

You wouldn't know just from the swing in their
step,
the ear to ear smile, that there's more to the
briefcase
than just knowledge. The Promethean gates are a
sacred
threshold. On one side burns enlightenment- it's
positive,
engaged. Turn the cheek and it's different-
darker,
multifaceted, non-archetypal and therefore less
palatable.
Like spies, there's so much to them that goes
unseen.
Failed relationships, drinking and planning. Oh,
and
don't forgot the mental illness. Living in a box is
claustrophobic; there's less air, no space to
stretch
out of the old roots. Harsh when all you do is
water
little trees- sun showers of care. And yet, the
moment
they walk through the gates you can always
expect

that swing in their step, and that ear to ear smile.

17

Front Porch

On our front porch, sweet eucalyptus scents
from ghost gums amid rosella plumage.
Below bygone verandas in incensed
liberty; Hyperion's patronage.

Juxtaposed porcelain, black bitterness,
cereal bowls. Imperfection's content
malcontent. Politics, books and Paris,
contentious yet mutual agreement.

Centuries of suffering Adam's curse,
nostalgic lost paradise of Eden.
Eve's apple begot knowledge of illness
but, like Pandora, blight begot fortune.

Like warm keys in locks, fingers interspersed,
on our front porch, the iron curse reversed.

Little Red Shoes

The little girl clutches at her mother's hand in the updraft,
twirling around in her little red shoes like a toy
ballerina.
All the girl can imagine are the ballet steps-
pirouette upon
pirouette- as if her romantic mind was tied by
marionette laces.
The girl looks up at her mother who hushes
reverence into her
and marks her face with the holy Trinity.
Curious but compliant,
she copies her mother. The Danube is cold this
morning. Hunks
of ice float lamentably against the current like
rebellious toy boats.
Only now does she notice the shoes. But where
are their owners?
With an arabesque, she reaches for something
too high for her.
Little red shoes- red with rust like dried blood.
Red like hers.
But not the same style- heels like her mother's.

Memory

The pillow soaks up my old wounds like a
bandage.
Each night the wet sponge howls of its
marinade-
memories of a dead me and strangely profound
wisdom.
They say children's stories are the most potent,
their meaning modest-
acute like a pin prick- weighty like a boulder.
Some daydreams are still sore, some laughable,
all a wall to the dark.

Facade

The crocodile blows a cigarette façade. His maw
chomps terrible phrases,
his leathery tail swats a riposte. Yet the scales
are so easily penetrated;
strangely so for someone so frightful.
Suddenly the scales peel like old stickers- rusted
like mail. The sinew runs
and cowers like a whimpering dog-
dehumanised as he too dehumanised.
He made the mask of labels- but the façade is
made of crystal inventions.

Snake skin

Conversations with my youth. Did you know
that we'd turn out this way?
You always liked pirates, cars and dinosaurs-
you'd play pretend for days
without a pause.

Nostalgia tastes ephemeral, fleeting, intoxicating
like a stiff drink. But life
changed and so did we. It got taller, grew a
looming shadow like a bully.
It stole the toys with harsh experiences and
glass-shard hearts.
In the tears we were reborn, an anti-phoenix, or
split like a moon-
a little light a little dark- changeable as the tides.
Old friend, I am sorry
that you had to be shed like a snake skin, though
you still hug me
tight in my night castle of delights- where
pirates, cars and dinosaurs play.

Breathing under water

It's a strange sensation, craven, and as odd as breathing under water. Why did the forbearers spin such tales, weave such intricate tapestries? Pull at a thread and the whole rug soon frays. It gets messy like dead roots, draining fervour from the passenger passers-by. Watch them catch their merry little trains.
How boring to bear that angst. So cliché, silly, even. Frivolous. And yet, what a wonderful life it would be to fly, but someone once said we couldn't. The shoes are made of stone, weighed down by worn hardbacks and Stone Age narratives. But humans still see their angel wings- begrudging flightless birds.
Meaning- she's flippant and fleeting. She wants you to chase, to bite, to bide, but when you hug her she's vapour. No amour, nevermore, nevermore. The siren was kind for a time; shame we made them up. Even so, maybe it's fine to sit on the bench, let the passengers meet their stops. Just sit on the bench.